WITH EXTREME AWKWARDNESS AND NO SMALL amount of embarrassment, we would like to apologize for destroying your restaurant. We know it looks as if a disgruntled hard rock band just left, but, the truth is, we're only an average family. If, during the excavation, you find you need to call in the HazMat crew, please do send us the bill. Again, we are sorry and promise not to return with our baby for at least the next few months.

SORRY

IT IS TO ENGAGE IN SEVERE UNDERSTATEMENT to suggest that things have been a bit amplified on our side of the fence lately. The 3 A.M. crying has become extraordinary. In fact, it probably comes as little surprise to you to learn that we've been contacted by the FBI about putting our baby's eardrum-busting cry on loudspeakers for use in standoffs with militia compounds. We are so very sorry. Your complimentary earplugs will arrive shortly.

SORRY

DEPENDING ON YOUR RESPECTIVE TOLERANCE for unremitting, ear-piercing screaming, you're probably relieved that our travel together is finally, mercifully over. We do wish to apologize for our baby's pushing the needle to decibels that make ear doctors start handing out pamphlets. But please know that this minor setback will not keep us from striving to be as perfect and happy as the model family pictured on the box our car seat came in. We hope we will be closer to that goal, should our paths cross again.

SORRY

IT IS WITH MUCH APOLOGY THAT WE HAVE momentarily suspended our principles and left a used diaper in this public trash can. Those of you with weak constitutions should know that said diaper's malodorous strength, achieved at full maturation, is truly phenomenal and should be avoided. Also, we have kindly written our address on the back so that the Army Corps of Engineers can send us an environmental-impact statement.

SORRY

THERE ARE REPERCUSSIONS, SERIOUS REPERCUSSIONS to fatherhood. Chiefly my apparent loss of masculinity. And for that I apologize. But what's a Dad to do with the necessary employment of words such as "onesie" and "binky" and "blankie"? And since when did I start talking in glass-shattering goo-goo octaves or doing that highly embarrassing, exaggerated, fingers-spread-out "Yaaay" clap in front of the baby? I'm so sorry. It's probably just a phase.

SORRY

IF I'VE LEARNED ONE THING IN MY INITIAL TIME as a parent, it's that I owe you, my partner in this venture, some apologies. One for engaging in that back-and-forth opera of semi-conscious snorts and moans to suggest I was still asleep when the baby started crying at 4 A.M. One for figuring out our baby's pooping schedule so that "my turn" always falls on a pee diaper. And one for passing out right before our long-awaited "date night."

SORRY

AS IT TURNS OUT, YES, WE ARE STILL ALIVE.

We apologize for not staying in touch with you and our other single friends, it's just that parenting has us rejiggering our priorities. But you wouldn't want to hang out with us right now anyway. We talk nonstop about our baby, make siren sounds every time a fire truck goes by, and hyper-sterilize everything. But hey, do call us though—we could really use some news from the outside world. Or, call us after you've found someone, married, and had your baby.

SORRY

HERE'S AN UNDERSTATEMENT: I THINK MY BABY is cuter than yours. I think my child is in higher percentiles across the board. I think my baby is more alert than yours, will walk sooner than yours, talk sooner than yours, and will get that final day care spot ahead of yours. For such offending thoughts, I would apologize. But that sort of thing would be beside the point. Because you're most certainly thinking the same thing about your own baby.

SORRY

AMONG THE MANY THOUSANDS OF THINGS parenthood has made me suddenly fall behind on, one is writing you a timely thank-you note. And I am so sorry. Because not only has your kind gift made our baby the envy of the local stroller fashionistas, it has also served as a building block for our little one's mental development. But you see, every time I sit down to write you, I end up...wait, the baby's crying. I have to go. Sorry.

SORRY

OKAY, OKAY, I KNOW I'VE BEEN CALLING

your house so much you'd think I was trying to be the tenth lucky caller or something. I'm sorry. It's just that this whole parenting/breastfeeding/nurturing thing seemed so much easier when you had your baby. I mean, I've actually seen you smiling with your baby. And I think your hair even gets brushed. I must be doing something wrong. Anyway, please don't put me on your Caller ID Rejection List.

SORRY

ONE OF THE LEAST FORTUNATE REALITIES OF parentdom is the sudden and perplexing shift in our driving style. And to you, fellow motorists, we apologize. Sure, we now drive at a cautious speed not dissimilar to a funeral procession. And sure, our car is loaded up with so much baby gear that we look like a west-heading truck in *The Grapes of Wrath*. But Baby's on Board. And hey, you try driving while doing the blind "reach back" for a lost pacifier.

SORRY

IT WOULD BE NEARLY IMPOSSIBLE TO OVERSTATE my current level of fatigue. And for that, my poor body, I apologize. While I do adhere to the Surgeon General's mandate of eight hours of sleep (when jointly accounted over a period of three days), I know I am treating you poorly, like a tetherball that gets whacked violently just as it's about to come to a stop. No longer do I get tired; I am tired. And you have every right to retaliate by making me look like I've been camping in my backyard for the last week.

SORRY

WHAT, YOU MAY BE PARDONED FOR WONDERING, are we doing home so early? Yes, we realize we hired you to watch our baby for a few hours. And yes, we realize that our coming home after ten minutes because "The movie was sold out," or because "Silly us, the Tuesday Night Buffet is really on Wednesday night," or because "My husband swore the sky was falling" is sensationally transparent. We're so sorry. And we promise never to call you to baby-sit again.

SORRY

OH, SWEET MOTHER OF MERCY, PLEASE FORGIVE ME.
For I have just broken Parenting Rule Number One: No matter what (even if the Chicago Cubs win it all, even if the Prize Patrol Van pulls up in the driveway, even if the Horsemen of the Apocalypse are out front letting their horses drink from our birdbath), one should never, ever wake a sleeping baby. I knew this. I tried to be quiet. I'm so sorry. Apparently my degree of stealthiness leaves much to be desired.

SORRY

WITH EXTREME AWKWARDNESS AND NO SMALL amount of embarrassment, we would like to apologize for destroying your restaurant. We know it looks as if a disgruntled hard rock band just left, but, the truth is, we're only an average family. If, during the excavation, you find you need to call in the HazMat crew, please do send us the bill. Again, we are sorry and promise not to return with our baby for at least the next few months.

SORRY

IT IS TO ENGAGE IN SEVERE UNDERSTATEMENT to suggest that things have been a bit amplified on our side of the fence lately. The 3 A.M. crying has become extraordinary. In fact, it probably comes as little surprise to you to learn that we've been contacted by the FBI about putting our baby's eardrum-busting cry on loudspeakers for use in standoffs with militia compounds. We are so very sorry. Your complimentary earplugs will arrive shortly.

SORRY

DEPENDING ON YOUR RESPECTIVE TOLERANCE for unremitting, ear-piercing screaming, you're probably relieved that our travel together is finally, mercifully over. We do wish to apologize for our baby's pushing the needle to decibels that make ear doctors start handing out pamphlets. But please know that this minor setback will not keep us from striving to be as perfect and happy as the model family pictured on the box our car seat came in. We hope we will be closer to that goal, should our paths cross again.

SORRY

IT IS WITH MUCH APOLOGY THAT WE HAVE momentarily suspended our principles and left a used diaper in this public trash can. Those of you with weak constitutions should know that said diaper's malodorous strength, achieved at full maturation, is truly phenomenal and should be avoided. Also, we have kindly written our address on the back so that the Army Corps of Engineers can send us an environmental-impact statement.

SORRY

IT APPEARS TIMELINESS HAS ITSELF A NEWFOUND enemy. We refer, of course, to ourselves—since once again we have arrived over thirty minutes late. And for that we apologize. It's just that we're currently destabilized by excessive amounts of responsibility compounded by excessive amounts of sleep deprivation, complicated by the need for excessive amounts of gear. And simply getting out the door is a production rivaled only by circuses moving to the next town.

SORRY

THERE ARE REPERCUSSIONS, SERIOUS REPERCUSSIONS to fatherhood. Chiefly my apparent loss of masculinity. And for that I apologize. But what's a Dad to do with the necessary employment of words such as "onesie" and "binky" and "blankie"? And since when did I start talking in glass-shattering goo-goo octaves or doing that highly embarrassing, exaggerated, fingers-spread-out "Yaaay" clap in front of the baby? I'm so sorry. It's probably just a phase.

SORRY

IF I'VE LEARNED ONE THING IN MY INITIAL TIME as a parent, it's that I owe you, my partner in this venture, some apologies. One for engaging in that back-and-forth opera of semi-conscious snorts and moans to suggest I was still asleep when the baby started crying at 4 A.M. One for figuring out our baby's pooping schedule so that "my turn" always falls on a pee diaper. And one for passing out right before our long-awaited "date night."

SORRY

AS IT TURNS OUT, YES, WE ARE STILL ALIVE.

We apologize for not staying in touch with you and our other single friends, it's just that parenting has us rejiggering our priorities. But you wouldn't want to hang out with us right now anyway. We talk nonstop about our baby, make siren sounds every time a fire truck goes by, and hyper-sterilize everything. But hey, do call us though—we could really use some news from the outside world. Or, call us after you've found someone, married, and had your baby.

SORRY

HERE'S AN UNDERSTATEMENT: I THINK MY BABY is cuter than yours. I think my child is in higher percentiles across the board. I think my baby is more alert than yours, will walk sooner than yours, talk sooner than yours, and will get that final day care spot ahead of yours. For such offending thoughts, I would apologize. But that sort of thing would be beside the point. Because you're most certainly thinking the same thing about your own baby.

SORRY

AMONG THE MANY THOUSANDS OF THINGS parenthood has made me suddenly fall behind on, one is writing you a timely thank-you note. And I am so sorry. Because not only has your kind gift made our baby the envy of the local stroller fashionistas, it has also served as a building block for our little one's mental development. But you see, every time I sit down to write you, I end up...wait, the baby's crying. I have to go. Sorry.

SORRY

OKAY, OKAY, I KNOW I'VE BEEN CALLING

your house so much you'd think I was trying to be the tenth lucky caller or something. I'm sorry. It's just that this whole parenting/breastfeeding/nurturing thing seemed so much easier when you had your baby. I mean, I've actually seen you smiling with your baby. And I think your hair even gets brushed. I must be doing something wrong. Anyway, please don't put me on your Caller ID Rejection List.

SORRY

ONE OF THE LEAST FORTUNATE REALITIES OF parentdom is the sudden and perplexing shift in our driving style. And to you, fellow motorists, we apologize. Sure, we now drive at a cautious speed not dissimilar to a funeral procession. And sure, our car is loaded up with so much baby gear that we look like a west-heading truck in *The Grapes of Wrath*. But Baby's on Board. And hey, you try driving while doing the blind "reach back" for a lost pacifier.

SORRY

IT WOULD BE NEARLY IMPOSSIBLE TO OVERSTATE my current level of fatigue. And for that, my poor body, I apologize. While I do adhere to the Surgeon General's mandate of eight hours of sleep (when jointly accounted over a period of three days), I know I am treating you poorly, like a tetherball that gets whacked violently just as it's about to come to a stop. No longer do I get tired; I am tired. And you have every right to retaliate by making me look like I've been camping in my backyard for the last week.

SORRY

WHAT, YOU MAY BE PARDONED FOR WONDERING, are we doing home so early? Yes, we realize we hired you to watch our baby for a few hours. And yes, we realize that our coming home after ten minutes because "The movie was sold out," or because "Silly us, the Tuesday Night Buffet is really on Wednesday night," or because "My husband swore the sky was falling" is sensationally transparent. We're so sorry. And we promise never to call you to baby-sit again.

SORRY

OH, SWEET MOTHER OF MERCY, PLEASE FORGIVE ME.
For I have just broken Parenting Rule Number One: No matter what (even if the Chicago Cubs win it all, even if the Prize Patrol Van pulls up in the driveway, even if the Horsemen of the Apocalypse are out front letting their horses drink from our birdbath), one should never, ever wake a sleeping baby. I knew this. I tried to be quiet. I'm so sorry. Apparently my degree of stealthiness leaves much to be desired.

SORRY